Adult Colorir

ISBN-13: 978-1-940282-91-6

© Copyright 2016. All rights reserved. No part of this publication may be reproduced without the consent of the owner.
Tip Top Education.

Grab your coloring pencils or crayons.
Sit back. And relax.

You will love this adult
coloring book.
It's simply beautiful.

Beautiful Gardens

Floral animals

Peace and Relaxation

Inside you will find amazing drawings of beautiful flowers, floral designs, and graceful animals.

Each relaxing coloring page is located on the right side of the coloring book; the left side is blank, leaving it free for you to create relaxing drawings of your own, journal your thoughts, or simply leave as is.

It's your time...

Sample Images...

Made in the USA
Middletown, DE
05 August 2017